THE
Totally Awesome
BOOK OF USELESS
INFORMATION

Noel Botham

Illustrations by Travis Nichols

A PERIGEE BOOK

A PERIGEE BOOK
Published by the Penguin Group
Penguin Group (USA) Inc.
375 Hudson Street, New York, New York 10014, USA

Penguin Group (Canada), 90 Eglinton Avenue East, Suite 700, Toronto, Ontario M4P 2Y3, Canada (a division of Pearson Penguin Canada Inc.) · Penguin Books Ltd., 80 Strand, London WC2R 0RL, England · Penguin Group Ireland, 25 St. Stephen's Green, Dublin 2, Ireland (a division of Penguin Books Ltd.) · Penguin Group (Australia), 250 Camberwell Road, Camberwell, Victoria 3124, Australia (a division of Pearson Australia Group Pty. Ltd.) · Penguin Books India Pvt. Ltd., 11 Community Centre, Panchsheel Park, New Delhi—110 017, India · Penguin Group (NZ), 67 Apollo Drive, Rosedale, Auckland 0632, New Zealand (a division of Pearson New Zealand Ltd.) · Penguin Books (South Africa) (Pty.) Ltd., 24 Sturdee Avenue, Rosebank, Johannesburg 2196, South Africa Penguin Books Ltd., Registered Offices: 80 Strand, London WC2R 0RL, England

While the author has made every effort to provide accurate telephone numbers and Internet addresses at the time of publication, neither the publisher nor the author assumes any responsibility for errors, or for changes that occur after publication. Further, publisher does not have any control over and does not assume any responsibility for author or third-party websites or their content.

First edition: June 2012

Library of Congress Cataloging-in-Publication Data

Botham, Noel. 1940–
The totally awesome book of useless information / Noel Botham ;
illustrations by Travis Nichols.
p.   cm.
"A Perigee book."
ISBN 978-0-399-15925-1
1. Curiosities and wonders.   2. Handbooks, vade-mecums, etc.   I. Nichols, Travis.
II. Useless Information Society.   III. Useless Information Society.   IV. Title.
AG243.B6638 2012
031.02—dc23   2012002186

PRINTED IN THE UNITED STATES OF AMERICA
22nd Printing

ALWAYS LEARNING   PEARSON

THE
Totally Awesome
BOOK OF USELESS
INFORMATION

Squirrels can climb trees faster than they can run on the ground.

"Happy Birthday to You" is the most often sung song in America.

A bumblebee beats its wings about 160 times a second.

Sleeping Beauty slept for one hundred years.

Queen Elizabeth I had more than two thousand dresses.

More presidents have been born in the state of Virginia than any other state.

Sharks are the only fish that can blink with both eyes.

Christopher Columbus had blond hair.

A starfish doesn't have a brain.

The oldest-known goldfish lived to forty-one years of age. Its name was Fred.

The most money that can be lost in one turn in Monopoly is $5,070.

One in every four Americans has appeared on television.

Mel Blanc, the voice of Bugs Bunny, wasn't a fan of raw carrots.

An iguana can hold its breath for twenty-eight minutes.

Crocodiles cannot stick
their tongues out.

President John Quincy Adams owned a pet alligator, which he kept in the East Room of the White House.

A pig always sleeps on its side.

Scooby-Doo's real first name is Scoobert. Shaggy's real first name is Norville.

Mosquitoes are more attracted to the color blue than any other color.

Mickey Mouse was the first nonhuman to win an Oscar.

There are 225 spaces on a Scrabble board.

Bees must visit around five thousand flowers to make a spoonful of honey.

People in Iceland read more books per capita than any other people in the world.

In the United States, 12,500 puppies are born every hour.

Dalmatians are born pure white. Their spots don't begin to appear until after they are born.

The longest Monopoly game ever played was 1,680 hours (seventy days). The longest Monopoly game in a bathtub was ninety-nine hours long.

Telephonophobia is the fear of telephones.

Cats have four rows of whiskers.

Arachibutyrophobia is the fear of peanut butter sticking to the roof of your mouth.

Rats can tread water for three days without stopping.

The tallest man on record was 8 feet, 11.1 inches tall.

Venus and Uranus are the only planets that rotate clockwise.

The only insect that can turn its head is a praying mantis.

The world's longest name is Adolph Blaine
Charles David Earl Frederick Gerald Hubert
Irvin John Kenneth Lloyd Martin Nero Oliver
Paul Quincy Randolph Sherman Thomas
Uncas Victor William Xerxes Yancy Zeus
Wolfeschlegelsteinhausenbergerdorft Sr.

The tallest mammal is the giraffe.

The human brain stops growing at the age
of eighteen.

The world's tallest mountains, the
Himalayas, are growing about 2.4 inches
taller every year.

The female lion does more than 90 percent
of the hunting, not the male.

Termites eat through wood
twice as fast when listening
to rock music.

The Bible is the most
shoplifted book in America.

Rhinos belong to the same family as horses and are thought to have inspired the myth of the unicorn.

The gap between two upper front teeth is called diastema.

The night vision of tigers is six times better than that of humans.

A horologist measures time.

A baby panda is smaller than a mouse when it is born.

Fingernails grow nearly four times faster than toenails.

A fox's tail is called a brush.

Your thumb is the same length as your nose.

Spain literally means "the land of rabbits."

Identical twins do not have identical fingerprints.

The killer whale is not actually a whale but is the largest member of the dolphin family.

The world's largest shopping mall (by total area) is in China, but has been 99 percent vacant since opening. Some of its features are a canal with gondolas and an indoor-outdoor roller coaster.

The average person blinks more than ten million times a year.

A rat can last longer without water than a camel.

The word *karate* means "empty hand."

To see at night as well as an owl, you would need eyeballs as big as grapefruits.

A sneeze travels out of your mouth at more than one hundred miles per hour.

It is impossible to sneeze with your eyes open.

The largest ever jack-o'-lantern was carved from a 1,469-pound pumpkin on Halloween 2005.

The most difficult tongue
twister is "The sixth sick
Sheik's sixth sheep's sick."

The ostrich has only two toes.

The oldest word in the English language is *town*.

There are 450 hairs in an average eyebrow.

Diet Coke was invented in 1982.

"I am" is the shortest complete sentence in the English language.

The faces on Mount Rushmore are sixty feet tall. They are of presidents George Washington, Thomas Jefferson, Theodore Roosevelt, and Abraham Lincoln.

The most used letter in the English alphabet is E; Q is the least used.

In England in the 1880s, *pants* was considered a dirty word.

Rats can't vomit.

Men get hiccups more often than women do.

No word in the English language rhymes with *month, orange, silver,* or *purple.*

Women blink twice as often as men do.

Lightning strikes the ground about six thousand times per minute.

November 19 is Have a Bad Day Day.

The most commonly used word in English conversation is *I*.

The largest school in the world is in the Philippines and has around twenty-five thousand students.

Ronald Reagan was the oldest man to be elected president of the United States.

Less than 2 percent of the water on Earth is fresh.

Most spiders have eight eyes.

About one-tenth of the world's surface is permanently covered in ice.

Pearls melt in vinegar.

Seven percent of Americans eat McDonald's every day.

The world's largest yo-yo is 1,625 pounds.

In Indiana, there is a town named Santa Claus.

A can of Diet Coke will float in water, while a can of regular Coke sinks.

Guinness World Records holds the record for the book most often stolen from public libraries.

Australia is the only continent without an active volcano.

Eating raw onions is good for unblocking a stuffed nose.

The penguin is the only bird that walks upright.

The peanut is a vegetable and a member of the pea family.

The world's heaviest man was more than 1,400 pounds.

French fries were invented in Belgium.

The average person laughs thirteen times a day.

The longest snake ever captured measured twenty-four feet.

In a lifetime, the average person in America spends eight years watching television.

The oldest known vegetable is the pea.

The Statue of Liberty's fingernails weigh about one hundred pounds each.

Tomatoes and cucumbers are fruits.

There is a house in New Jersey built in the shape of an elephant, a house in Oklahoma shaped like a chicken, and a house in Massachusetts made entirely of newspapers.

The largest cabbage ever grown weighed 125.9 pounds.

The most widely eaten fruit in America is the banana.

There are no penguins anywhere in the northern hemisphere except in zoos.

The Great Wall of China is the world's longest wall and runs for more than 4,000 miles. It took more than 1,700 years to build.

The heaviest sumo wrestler ever recorded weighed in at a thundering 560 pounds.

Grapes explode when you put them in the microwave.

A cucumber consists of 96 percent water.

John Hancock was the only one of the signers of the Declaration of Independence to actually sign it on the Fourth of July.

Thirty-five billion emails each day are sent throughout the world.

More than a third of all pineapples come from Hawaii.

The gray whale is not really gray. It is black.

Eyeglasses were invented in China.

There are an average of two earthquakes every minute in the world.

There are more brown M&M's in plain M&M's than in peanut M&M's.

The winters of 1911 and 1932 were so cold that Niagara Falls froze.

Benjamin Franklin invented the rocking chair.

There are more doughnut shops per capita in Canada than in any other country.

The shoelace was invented in England in 1790. Before then, all shoes were fastened with buckles.

Mickey Mouse's birthday is November 18.

There is a Historical
Museum of Spaghetti in
Pontedassio, Italy.

The most popular ice cream flavor is vanilla.

The flounder swims sideways.

The average American chews 190 sticks of gum, drinks 600 sodas and 800 gallons of water, and consumes 135 pounds of sugar and 19 pounds of cereal per year.

In Disney's *Cinderella*, Cinderella loses her left shoe at the ball.

Saturday night is the biggest night of the week for eating pizza.

Everyone is color-blind at birth.

More popcorn is sold in Dallas than anywhere else in the United States.

Ancient Egyptians believed eating fried mice would cure a toothache.

Two million different combinations of sandwiches can be created from a Subway menu.

Fingernails are made from the same substance as a bird's beak.

The chocolate chip cookie was invented in 1933.

A pair of human feet contains two hundred and fifty thousand sweat glands. There are about one trillion bacteria on each foot.

In the summer, walnuts
get a tan.

Turnips turn green when
sunburned.

The screwdriver was
invented before the screw.

In 1983, a Japanese artist made a copy of the *Mona Lisa* completely out of toast.

Fish can learn more quickly than dogs.

Ketchup originated in China.

Crickets hear through their knees.

Potato chips were invented in Louisiana in 1853.

The shortest president was James Madison at five feet, four inches.

Mosquitoes have teeth.

Beijing boasts the world's largest Kentucky Fried Chicken.

Sheep snore.

The largest apple pie ever baked was forty feet by twenty-three feet.

A squirrel's brain is approximately the size of a walnut.

It is estimated that Americans eat 10 million tons of turkey on Thanksgiving Day.

Chewing gum while peeling onions will keep you from crying.

For a deck of cards to be mixed up enough to play with properly, it should be shuffled at least seven times.

The pupil of an octopus's eye is rectangular.

More people use blue toothbrushes than red ones.

A man once had the hiccups for sixty-eight years.

The bestselling chocolate bar in Russia is Snickers.

Toilets in Australia flush counterclockwise.

A snowflake can take up to
an hour to fall from a cloud
to the surface of the Earth.

The largest pumpkin pie ever made weighed 3,699 pounds.

In 1825, the first toilet was installed in the White House.

The world's oldest piece of chewing gum is nine thousand years old.

The plastic things on the end of shoelaces are called aglets.

The peach was the first fruit eaten on the moon.

Most people button their shirts starting at the bottom.

Dunkin' Donuts serves about 112,500 doughnuts each day.

On average, humans fart once per hour.

The armhole in clothing is called an armsaye.

Jeans were named after Genoa, Italy, where the first denim cloth was made.

More than 189 billion Lego pieces in two thousand different shapes have been produced since the first one was made in 1949. This is enough for about thirty Lego pieces for every person on Earth.

The biggest-selling
restaurant food is
french fries.

The largest hamburger
in the world weighed in
at 777 pounds.

The world's longest carrot was a little more than nineteen feet.

There are more Barbie dolls in Italy than Canadians in Canada.

Dinosaur droppings are called coprolites.

Totally Hair Barbie is the best-selling Barbie of all time.

The habit of nose picking is called rhinotillexomania.

Slinkys were invented by an airplane mechanic.

Roosters cannot crow if they are not able to fully extend their necks.

Seven percent of Americans claim they never bathe.

If you took a standard Slinky and stretched it out, it would measure eighty-seven feet.

A total of 364 gifts are given in the song "The Twelve Days of Christmas."

Carrots are not always orange and can also be purple, white, red, or yellow.

In 1946, the first TV toy commercial aired. It was for Mr. Potato Head.

Seventy-five percent of people who play the car radio while driving also sing along to it.

The hundred billionth crayon made by Crayola was periwinkle blue.

In 1955, a book was returned to Cambridge University Library 288 years overdue.

The tomato is both the state vegetable and the state fruit of Arkansas.

When offered a new pen to write with, 97 percent of people will write their own name.

Rubber bands last longer when refrigerated.

Brontology is the study of thunder.

A Virginia law requires all bathtubs to be kept out in the yard, not inside the house.

The most landed-on squares in Monopoly are New York Avenue, Illinois Avenue, B&O Railroad, and Reading Railroad.

Celebrating Christmas was once illegal in England.

Japan has the world's largest bowling alley.

It's possible to lead a cow upstairs but not downstairs.

Thomas Edison, the inventor of the lightbulb, was afraid of the dark.

No two cornflakes look the
same.

Four thousand people
are injured by teapots
every year.

Forty thousand Americans
are injured by toilets
every year.

There are more than 980 species of bats.

There are eighteen different animal shapes in the Animal Crackers cookie zoo.

In Texas, it is illegal to put graffiti on someone else's cow.

Paper can be made from asparagus.

It is against the law to stare at the mayor of Paris.

Two-thirds of the world's eggplants are grown in New Jersey.

In Arizona, it is illegal to hunt camels.

China uses 45 billion chopsticks per year, using 25 million trees to make them.

In Sweden, it is illegal to train a seal to balance a ball on its nose.

A typical lightning bolt is only one inch wide and five miles long.

The world's largest watermelon weighed 268.8 pounds.

It would take eighty moons to equal the weight of the Earth.

Ancient Egyptians slept on pillows made of stone.

Farts have been clocked at a
speed of ten feet per second.

If you were to dig a hole from one side of the Earth to the other and jump into it, it would take about forty-two minutes to reach the opposite end. At that point you would fall back into the hole and repeat the trip back and forth forever.

Fortune cookies were invented in Los Angeles.

Babies like pretty faces better than plain ones.

Caesar salad was invented in Mexico.

Six-year-olds laugh an average of three hundred times a day.

Pilgrims ate popcorn at the first Thanksgiving.

There are more bacteria in the mouth than there are people in the world.

There are 294 or 296 steps to the top of the Leaning Tower of Pisa depending on which staircase you are climbing.

The city of Denver, Colorado, claims to have invented the cheeseburger.

It takes seventeen facial muscles to smile, but forty-two muscles to frown.

Shrimp swim backward.

Buckingham Palace has more than six hundred rooms.

The side of a hammer is
called a cheek.

Most people's legs are slightly different lengths.

Water is the official state beverage of Indiana.

The Eiffel Tower's height varies as much as six inches depending on the temperature, so it is shorter in the winter.

There is a town in Texas called Ding Dong.

The average person sheds more than eight pounds of skin each year.

Roast camel is sometimes served at Bedouin wedding feasts.

The San Diego Zoo has the largest collection of animals in the world.

The average human eyelash lives about 150 days.

Maine is the toothpick capital of the world.

The average eyeball weighs about one ounce.

A baseball has exactly 108 stitches.

On average, adults spend seventy-seven minutes eating per day.

In South Africa, termites are often roasted and eaten like pretzels or popcorn.

Baseball's home plate is seventeen inches wide.

Boys are more likely to be left-handed than girls are.

Bears that appear in movies can earn around $20,000 a day.

When two words are combined to form a new word (like breakfast + lunch = brunch), the new word is called a *portmanteau*.

It takes about eight seconds to make a baseball bat in a baseball bat factory.

Fear of spiders is the most common phobia, followed by fear of snakes.

People dream an average of five times a night.

Kite-flying is a professional sport in Thailand.

Baby squirrels are called "kittens."

The national sport of Japan is sumo wrestling.

Horses can sleep standing up.

A hockey puck is one inch thick.

A normal raindrop falls at about seven miles per hour.

Fish and snakes don't have eyelids.

It takes one fifteen- to twenty-year-old tree to produce seven hundred paper grocery bags.

Some spas in China offer fish pedicures, where live fish eat away the dead skin on the feet.

For every person on Earth, there are 200 million insects.

An iceberg contains more heat than a match.

Dogs do not have an appendix.

The smallest unit of time is the yoctosecond.

In Kentucky, it is illegal to carry ice cream in your back pocket.

In India, men can wear pajamas in public as they are standard daytime apparel.

Recycling one glass jar saves enough energy to power a TV for three hours.

Saying "rabbit, rabbit" upon waking the first day of every month is supposed to bring good luck for that month. If you forget to say it, say it backward or say "moose, moose" on the second day of the month.

The world's population grows by 100 million people each year.

A baby blue whale is twenty-five feet long at birth.

One in every five people lives in China.

A baby giraffe is about six feet tall at birth.

People who are lying tend to look up and to the left.

An estimated 80 percent of creatures on Earth have six legs.

A dragonfly has a life span of four to seven weeks.

Antarctica is the only land on the planet that is not owned by any country.

Butterflies taste with their hind feet.

Most burglaries occur in the
winter.

Panama is the only place in the world where someone can see the sun rise over the Pacific Ocean and set over the Atlantic.

The original name for the butterfly was the flutterby.

In London, it is illegal to drive a car without sitting in the front seat.

In Somalia, it has been decreed illegal to carry old chewing gum stuck on the tip of your nose.

Soccer is played in more countries than any other sport.

Frogs must close their eyes to swallow.

The average person speaks about 31,500 words a day.

In Arizona, donkeys are not allowed to sleep in bathtubs.

Toads don't have teeth, but frogs do.

The longest sustained fart was two minutes, forty-two seconds.

The maximum number of points that can be scored in the game Pac-Man is 3,333,360. The first time a perfect game was played was in 1999.

Pirates thought having an earring would improve their eyesight.

It is estimated that, within the entire universe, there are more than a trillion galaxies.

Dinosaurs lived on Earth for nearly 150 million years—seventy-five times longer than humans have now lived on Earth.

The first living creature to orbit the Earth was a dog named Laika in 1957.

The woolly mammoth had tusks almost sixteen feet long.

Some dinosaurs were as small as hens.

Light from the moon takes about a second and a half to reach Earth. The moon is about 238,000 miles away and is our closest neighbor.

Lions sleep up to twenty hours a day.

The cheetah can reach a speed of up to forty-five miles per hour in just two seconds.

The moon orbits Earth every 27.32 days.

The polar bear is the only bear that has hair on the soles of its feet. This protects the animal's feet from the cold and prevents slipping on the ice.

It takes food seven seconds
to travel from the mouth to
the stomach.

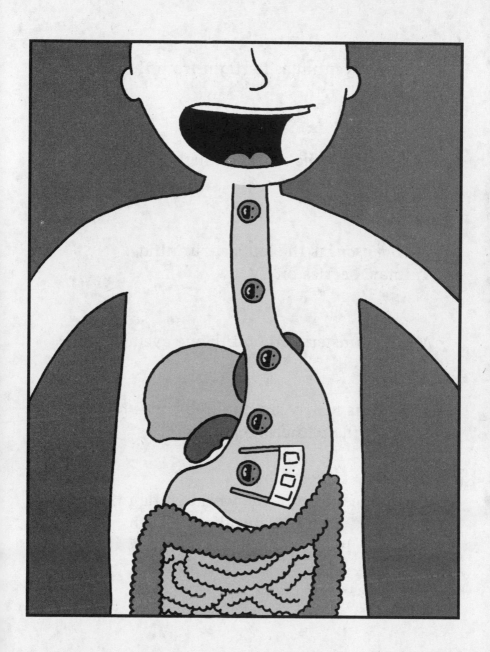

It takes 8.5 minutes for light from the sun to reach the Earth.

The mouse is the most common mammal in the United States.

The Simpsons is the longest-running animated series on TV.

Many hamsters only blink one eye at a time.

The sun is nearly six hundred times bigger than all the planets combined.

The loudest bird in the world is the male bellbird, found in Central and South America. It can be heard from miles away.

Bats always turn left when exiting a cave.

The magic word *abracadabra* was originally intended to be spoken to cure hay fever.

There are more than three hundred species of parrot.

A duck has three eyelids.

The sun produces more energy every minute than all the energy used on Earth in a whole year.

A sheep, a duck, and a rooster were the first passengers in a hot-air balloon.

The only person to ever play golf on the moon was astronaut Alan Shepard. His golf ball was never found.

Halley's Comet will next
appear in 2061.

Felix the Cat was the first cartoon character to be made into a parade balloon.

An ostrich's eye is bigger than its brain.

The most common set of initials for Superman's friends and enemies is L.L.

The hummingbird is the only bird that can fly backward.

Sitcom characters rarely say good-bye when they hang up the phone.

Flamingos can only eat with their heads upside down.

All the coal, oil, gas, and wood on Earth would keep the sun burning for only a few days.

The penguin is the only bird that can swim but not fly.

The Earth is not round. It is an oblate spheroid, meaning it is flattened at the poles and bulging at the equator.

Jellyfish are composed of more than 95 percent water and don't have a brain, heart, bones, or actual eyes.

Bert and Ernie on *Sesame Street* are named after characters in the classic movie *It's a Wonderful Life.*

If you yelled for eight years,
seven months, and six days,
you would have produced
enough sound energy to heat
a cup of coffee.

Dolphins swim in circles while they sleep, with the eye on the outside of the circle open to keep watch for predators. After a certain amount of time, they reverse and swim in the opposite direction with the opposite eye open.

The coldest place in the universe is something called the Boomerang Nebula, about five thousand light-years away.

It is illegal to swim in the Central Park reservoir in New York City.

Sharks can travel up to forty miles per hour.

Dolphins jump out of the water to conserve energy. It is easier to move through the air than through the water.

Hawaii's Mount Waialeale is the wettest place in the world. It rains about 90 percent of the year.

Some sharks swim in a figure eight when frightened.

Kermit the Frog is left-handed.

There once were more sea lions on Earth than people.

Astronauts get taller when
they are in space.

The farthest point from any ocean is in China.

There are more than one hundred million dogs and cats in the United States.

On at least two occasions, it has snowed in the Sahara Desert.

A geep is a cross between a goat and a sheep.

Reindeer like to eat bananas.

There is a town in West Virginia called Looneyville.

An armadillo can walk underwater.

Giant tortoises can live to be over 150 years old.

The state flag of Alaska was designed by a thirteen-year-old boy.

Children between the ages of two and seven color, on average, for twenty-eight minutes every day.

At their nearest point, Russia and America are less than three miles apart.

The mudskipper fish can actually walk on land.

The average adult spends about twelve minutes in the shower.

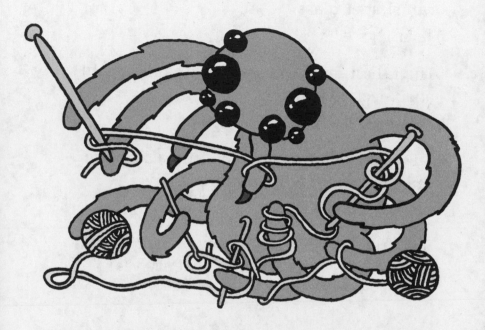

Tarantulas cannot spin webs.

The pistol shrimp makes a noise so loud it can shatter glass.

The tallest president was Abraham Lincoln at six feet, four inches.

The average four-year-old child asks more than four hundred questions a day.

Squirrels usually live longer in captivity than in the wild—fifteen or twenty years versus often only one year.

Every U.S. president has worn glasses or contact lenses.

Every U.S. president has had at least one sibling; none have been only children.

Tuna can swim at a steady rate of nine miles per hour for an indefinite period of time—and they never stop moving because they need a continual flow of water across their gills to breathe.

The world's smallest painting was painted onto a grain of corn.

It took Leonardo da Vinci twelve years to paint the *Mona Lisa*'s lips.

The most money that can be lost in one trip around a Monopoly board is $26,040.

Charlie Brown's father is a barber.

Bats are the only mammals
that can fly.

Sixty-six percent of Americans admit to reading in the bathroom.

Dr. Seuss pronounced his name so it would rhyme with *rejoice*.

The last word in the Bible is *Amen*.

There is no such thing as blue food—even blueberries are purple.

Clinophobia is the fear of going to bed.

A funambulist is another name for a tightrope walker.

The two ends of a magnet are called poles.

Presidents Thomas Jefferson, John Adams, and James Monroe all died on the Fourth of July.

Goofy's son is named Goofy Jr.

The first movie theater charged a nickel for admission. It opened in 1905.

Paedophobia is the fear of children.

President Andrew Johnson sometimes made his own clothes.

Mozart wrote his own melody to the nursery rhyme "Twinkle, Twinkle, Little Star" at the age of five.

Tigers have striped skin, not
just striped fur.

Every day more money is printed for
Monopoly than by the U.S. Treasury.

Mariah Carey's favorite food is pizza.

Punctuation didn't exist in writing until the
fifteenth century.

President William Taft once got stuck in his
bathtub.

The Queen of England has two birthdays—
one real and one official.

Tonsurphobia is the fear of haircuts.

People used to say "ahoy" instead of "hello" when they answered the phone.

The Old English word for *sneeze* is *fneosam*.

Peanuts characters Linus and Lucy have another brother named Rerun.

The word *coward* originally referred to a boy who took care of cows.

The letter *W* is the only letter in the alphabet that has more than one syllable.

The longest word in the English language is 1,909 letters long and refers to a part of DNA.

It would take 3.6 billion
people holding hands
to reach all the way around
the sun.

Justin Bieber's favorite food is spaghetti and meatballs.

All dogs are descendents of wolves.

There are only twelve letters in the Hawaiian alphabet.

Maine is the only state whose name is only one syllable.

There are believed to be more than six thousand different languages spoken on Earth.

No Spanish words begin with the letter W.

The most common name in Italy is Mario Rossi.

Four hundred quarter-pounder hamburgers can be made out of one cow.

The longest one-syllable word in the English language is *screeched*.

Coca-Cola was originally green.

Actor Tom Hanks is related to Abraham Lincoln.

It takes more than five hundred peanuts to make one twelve-ounce jar of peanut butter.

Jaguars are scared of dogs.

The only real food U.S. astronauts are allowed in space are pecans.

Bookkeeper and *bookkeeping* are the only words in the English language with three consecutive double letters.

Pomology is the study of fruit.

Doughnuts originated in Holland.

Mickey Mouse's ears are always turned to the front, no matter which direction his head is pointing.

The sandwich was invented by and named after the Earl of Sandwich.

Donald Duck's middle name is Fauntleroy. His sister is named Dumbella.

The most milk a single cow can produce is 55,849 gallons.

There are one hundred squares on a Snakes and Ladders board.

Dorothy's ruby slippers from the movie *The Wizard of Oz* were once auctioned off for $165,000.

The most popular pizza topping in Australia is eggs. In Chile, it is mussels and clams. In America, it is pepperoni.

An octopus will eat its own
arms if it gets really hungry.

The Adventures of Tom Sawyer was the first novel written on a typewriter.

The world's largest ketchup bottle is 170 feet tall.

Astronauts are not allowed to eat beans before they go into space because passing wind in a space suit damages it.

The words *racecar* and *kayak* are palindromes, meaning they're spelled the same whether they're read left to right or right to left.

Salt is the only rock humans can eat.

The face of a penny can hold thirty drops of water.

The first pennies minted in the United States were inscribed with the motto "Mind your own business."

Barbie's full name is Barbara Millicent Roberts.

The Popsicle was invented by an eleven-year-old boy.

Pac-Man was originally going to be called Puck Man.

The yo-yo was originally used as a hunting weapon.

The elephant is the only
mammal that can't jump.

The average pencil can write approximately fifty thousand English words.

In Helsinki, Finland, instead of giving parking tickets, the police usually deflate tires.

The Egyptian pharaoh Ramses II had iii sons and 67 daughters.

In California, it is illegal to eat oranges while bathing.

The ancient Romans liked to eat flamingo tongues.

Every citizen of Kentucky is required by law to take a bath at least once a year.

In Omaha, Nebraska, it's against the law to burp or sneeze in church.

A woman in Los Angeles once married a rock.

Honey is the only food that doesn't spoil.

In ancient Egypt, killing a cat was a crime punishable by death.

Five jelly flavors that flopped: celery, coffee, cola, apple, and chocolate.

During one lifetime the average person eats sixty thousand pounds of food—the weight of six elephants.

It would take more than 150 million years to drive a car to the sun.

Two hundred million M&M's are sold every day in the United States.

A two-hundred-year-old piece of cheese was once sold for $1,513.

In a town in Canada, it is illegal to frown at cows.

About five hundred million years ago, a day only lasted 20.6 hours instead of 24.

The world's youngest parents were eight and nine and lived in China in 1910.

Before World War II, when guards were posted at the fence, anyone could walk up to the front door of the White House.

A shrimp's heart is in its head.

During World War II, Americans trained
bats to drop bombs.

Monopoly games were used to smuggle items
into enemy camps during World War II.

Hershey bars were used as currency in some
countries during World War II.

Benjamin Franklin once designed an $8 bill.

Before the 1800s, there were no separately
designed shoes for right and left feet.

Caterpillars have about four
thousand muscles. Humans
have only about six hundred.

Up until 2006, there were officially nine planets in our solar system. That year Pluto was changed to a dwarf planet, so now there are only eight planets in the solar system.

Russian men used to be taxed for growing a beard.

The shortest war in history was between England and Zanzibar in 1896 and lasted thirty-eight minutes.

Leif Erikson, not Christopher Columbus, was the first European to set foot in North America.

Native Americans never actually ate turkey, even at Thanksgiving.

Alligators cannot move backward.

In Idaho, it is illegal to fish on a camel's back.

A group of rhinos is called a crash.

The Japanese national anthem has the oldest lyrics, from the ninth century.

It is physically impossible for pigs to look up at the sky.

The oldest bridge still used in the United States was built in 1697.

Gorillas often sleep for up to fourteen hours a day.

The Empire State Building has 6,500 windows.

The most common name for
a goldfish is Jaws.

No building in Washington, DC, can be built taller than the Washington Monument.

In Connecticut, in order for a pickle to officially be considered a pickle, it must bounce.

The Statue of Liberty's mouth is three feet wide.

The names of the two stone lions in front of the New York Public Library are Patience and Fortitude.

There aren't any clocks in Las Vegas casinos.

In Massachusetts, gorillas are not allowed in the backseat of a car.

The longest recorded
sneezing fit lasted 978 days.

The longest place name in the world is a hill in New Zealand called

Taumatawhakatangihangaoauauotameteaturipukakapikimaungahoronukupokaiwhenuakitanatahu.

Japan has 3,900 islands.

The Romans were the first people to exchange presents at Christmas.

Boxing is the most popular sport to create a film about.

Karate originated in India.

At any time, there are eighteen hundred thunderstorms in progress over the Earth's atmosphere.

All the stars in the Milky Way revolve around the center of the galaxy every two hundred million years.

Accounting for time zone differences, Santa Claus has thirty-one hours to deliver gifts on Christmas Eve, but that still means he has to visit 823 homes per second.

The tail section of an airplane gives the bumpiest ride.

A large, flawless emerald is worth more than a similarly large, flawless diamond.

Bamboo is the world's tallest grass.

Mercury is the only metal that is liquid at room temperature.

Because of the rotation of the Earth, an object can be thrown farther if it is thrown west.

A jiffy is equal to one-hundredth of a second, which is where the saying, "I'll be there in a jiffy!" comes from.

It takes forty-two days for an ostrich egg to hatch.

It can take more than two days for a chick to break out of its shell.

The Asiatic elephant takes over twenty months to give birth.

Earth is traveling through space at 660,000 miles per hour.

The leech has thirty-two brains.

A species of earthworm in Australia grows up to ten feet in length.

The harmonica is the world's
most popular instrument.

Some ribbon worms will eat themselves if they can't find food.

If you attempted to count the stars in a galaxy at a rate of one every second, it would take around three thousand years to count them all.

After eating, the housefly regurgitates its food and eats it again.

Grasshoppers have green blood.

South Africa produces two-thirds of the world's gold.

Mosquitoes are attracted to people who have recently eaten bananas.

Clouds fly higher during the day than at night.

Bees do not have ears.

The right lung takes in more air than the left lung.

Bees have five eyes: three small eyes on the top of a bee's head and two larger ones in front.

Spider silk is stronger than steel.

The human tooth has about fifty-five miles of canals in it.

The planet Saturn has a
density lower than water so,
if there was a bathtub large
enough to hold it, Saturn
would float.

The tongue is the only muscle in the human body that is only attached at one end.

Frogs move faster than toads.

Babies are born without kneecaps.

The white area at the base of a fingernail is called the lunula.

The skin that peels off after a sunburn is called blype.

Frogs drink and breathe through their skin.

The straw was invented by ancient Egyptians.

Bats cannot walk because their leg bones are too thin.

The single dot over the lowercase letter *i* is called a tittle.

Left-handed people cannot write Mandarin Chinese.

Basilisks can run on water.

People in Japan eat fried chicken and strawberry shortcake on Christmas Eve.

The scientific name for a gorilla is *Gorilla gorilla gorilla*.

Pound for pound,
hamburgers cost more than
new cars.

In ancient Greece, writing had no space between the words.

South Africa has eleven official languages.

Singapore is the only country with only one train station.

Moose have very bad vision. They sometimes mistake cars for other moose.

Butter is naturally white. Its yellow color is artificial.

Bats eat as many as six hundred bugs per hour.

JELL-O is the official state snack of Utah.

The longest lizard in the world is the Komodo dragon, at ten feet long.

The only continent without reptiles or snakes is Antarctica.

A "vamp" is the upper front top of a shoe.

Pigs can learn the same tricks dogs can in a shorter amount of time.

The first dinosaur appeared about 225 or 230 million years ago. It was called the Staurikosaurus, and it survived for about five million years.

Mr. Potato Head once got
four votes for mayor of Boise,
Idaho, in an election.

Napoleon Bonaparte was
afraid of cats.

Cranberries are sorted for
ripeness by bouncing them;
a fully ripened cranberry
can be dribbled like a
basketball.

The Oval Office is thirty-five feet long.

There is approximately one library book for every person on Earth.

A "keeper" is the loop on a belt that holds the loose end.

The most commonly misspelled word in the English language is *supersede*.

Almost half the newspapers in the world are published in the United States and Canada.

One out of every three American homes contains a Scrabble game.

Lime JELL-O gives off the same brain waves as adult humans when hooked up to an EEG machine.

A portrait of rapper Eminem was once created out of M&M's candies.

July is National Ice Cream Month.

Grasshoppers are the most popular insect snack in some parts of the world.

The average French citizen eats five hundred snails a year.

France eats the most cheese of any country, averaging 43.6 pounds per person per year.

A group of frogs is called
an army.

Tug-of-war used to be an
Olympic event.

The most cans of chicken noodle soup are
sold in January.

Some pumpkins can grow fifteen miles of
roots.

Onions, apples, and potatoes all have the
same taste. Their smells are what gives them
different flavors.

Tomatoes with a strawberry inside have
been successfully grown.

Urine was once used as a detergent for
washing.

Bamboo can grow three or four feet in one
day.

Dirty snow melts faster than white snow because it reflects less light.

The longest lightning bolt ever recorded was 118 miles long.

In China, there are six hundred bicycles for every car.

The Netherlands has the most bicycles in the world.

The world's longest escalator is in Hong Kong and rises 377 feet.

Some babies suck their thumb before they are born.

A Venus flytrap can eat a
whole cheeseburger.

It takes an average of forty-eight to one hundred tries to solve a Rubik's Cube puzzle. If done perfectly, any Rubik's Cube combination can be solved in seventeen turns.

One brow wrinkle is the result of two hundred thousand frowns.

The average person has about ten thousand taste buds.

Right-handed people tend to chew food on the right side of their mouths, and vice versa for left-handed people.

The brain is more active sleeping than it is watching TV.

One reason phone numbers are only seven digits (not including the area code) is because most people can only remember between five and nine digits in their short-term memory.

The human eye is constantly moving. It quivers thirty to fifty times per second.

The maximum heartbeat possible for a human is 220 beats per minute.

The human heart is about the size of a fist.

Men have more blood than women.

Tomatophagia is an eating disorder that causes people to crave things like ice, detergent, starch, clay, and dirt.

Synesthesia is a condition in which people can see speech, taste colors and shapes, and smell flavors.

One in three men picks his nose while driving.

The average person will walk far enough in a lifetime to go around the world four and a half times.

Ninety-nine percent of the life forms that have ever existed on Earth are extinct.

Turtles can breathe through their bottoms.

The world's longest cucumber was forty-seven inches.

There are twice as many chickens in the world as humans.

A cockroach's favorite food is the glue on the back of stamps.

The giant cricket of Africa enjoys eating human hair.

A deltiologist collects
postcards.

Cows can smell odors six miles away.

King Henry III of England kept pet lions in the Tower of London. He also once received a polar bear as a gift from the king of Norway and an elephant from the king of France.

Venice has four hundred bridges.

The Atlantic Ocean is the youngest of the world's oceans.

The world's largest alphabet is Cambodian, with seventy-four letters.

The Hundred Years' War actually lasted 116 years.

The world's largest gingerbread man weighed more than 1,308 pounds.

The first cloned mammal was Dolly the lamb, in 1996.

The first asteroid to be discovered is also the largest to be discovered so far, at six hundred miles long.

Comets speed up as they approach the sun and slow down as they move away from it.

Venus is brighter than any other planet and can sometimes be seen during the day.

All the planets in the solar system could be placed inside Jupiter.

The ancient Romans often
paid their taxes in honey.

In ancient Rome, it was considered a sign of leadership to be born with a crooked nose.

Maine was once known as the Earmuff Capital of the World since earmuffs were invented there.

The Tyrannosaurus Rex at the Field Museum in Chicago is named Sue.

Lions, leopards, tigers, and jaguars do not purr. They are also the only cat species that can roar.

Twinkies were originally called Little Shortcake Fingers.

Lobsters and grasshoppers cannot feel pain.

Dolphins do not breathe automatically like humans do.

New York was once called New Amsterdam.

Shark fossils have been found that are more than twice as old as dinosaur fossils.

Male sea lions sometimes go three months without eating.

The hippopotamus gives birth underwater but cannot swim.

Greenland has more ice on it than Iceland does, and Iceland has more grass and trees than Greenland.

Sheepdogs can smell forty-four times better than humans.

Elephants only get about two hours of sleep a day.

Twenty billion cards and packages are delivered every year in the United States between Thanksgiving and Christmas.

A rhinoceros's horn is made of compacted hair.

The only purple animal is the South African Blesbok.

The world's smallest mammal is the bumblebee bat of Thailand, which weighs less than a penny.

Camels have three eyelids to protect their eyes from blowing sand.

The giant African snail grows to a foot long.

The Oreo is the world's bestselling cookie.

The giant squid is the largest creature without a backbone. It can grow to fifty-five feet long. Each eye is a foot or more in diameter.

A giraffe moves both legs on one side of its body together when it runs.

The world's heaviest motorcycle weighed 10,470 pounds.

Texas is the only state that permits residents to vote from space.

Ancient Romans used urine
as an ingredient in
toothpaste.

The ice cream sundae was invented in 1875.

The giraffe's heart weighs twenty-five pounds and is two feet long.

Porcupines are excellent swimmers because their quills are hollow.

Jupiter has the most moons in the solar system—possibly as many as sixty-six.

Porcupines love salt.

Anteaters prefer termites to ants.

Woodpecker scalps, porpoise teeth, and giraffe tails have all been used as money.

The average person spends about two years on the phone in a lifetime.

The longest kiss on record lasted 417 hours.

Polar bear fur is not white, it's clear.

The world record for carrying a milk bottle on your head is twenty-four miles.

About one out of every seventy people who pick their nose actually eats their boogers.

August is the month when most babies are born.

The first fish in space was a guppy.

The ancient Egyptians
trained baboons to wait on
tables.

The world record for most children born to one mother is sixty-nine children.

Owls are the only birds that can see the color blue.

Bugs Bunny was originally called Happy Rabbit.

All female bees in a hive are sisters.

Artists had to draw more than six million spots for the Disney animated film *One Hundred and One Dalmatians.*

The longest recorded flight of a chicken was thirteen seconds.

The blood of an octopus is pale bluish green.

Most elephants weigh less than the tongue of the blue whale.

Mexico City sinks about ten inches a year.

An elephant's trunk can hold four gallons of water.

The dinosaur Brachiosaurus had a heart the size of a pickup truck.

Cows pass gas about sixteen times a day.

A lion's roar can be heard five miles away.

Thirty-five million pounds of candy corn is produced each year in America, which is enough to circle the moon nearly twenty-one times.

Each year the moon's orbit moves about one and a half inches father away from Earth.

No two lions have the same pattern of whiskers.

Wife-carrying is a sport in Finland.

The common garden worm has five pairs of hearts.

The longest Oscar awards ceremony was in 2000 and lasted 256 minutes.

There are more beetles than any other creature in the world.

The world's windiest place is Commonwealth Bay, Antarctica. Winds regularly exceed 150 miles per hour.

Slugs have twenty-seven thousand teeth.

The average meteor is no larger than a grain of sand.

A snail can sleep for three years.

Honeybees have hair on their eyes.

The only rock that floats in water is pumice.

Nose prints are the most reliable way of identifying dogs.

In the Caribbean, there are oysters that can climb trees.

Each year the Earth becomes about twelve tons heavier because of meteorites landing.

A 150-pound adult on Earth would weigh 250 tons on the sun.

The average human brain is 80 percent water.

There was once a U.S. state called Franklin, named after Benjamin Franklin. It eventually became part of Tennessee.

Argentina's name means "Land of Silver," but there is actually very little silver there.

The smallest church in the world is in Kentucky. It can hold three people.

Ostriches can run faster than horses.

Some polar bears turn green as a result of algae growing in their fur.

Dogs may be able to sense earthquakes before they happen.

The animals most likely to fall from the sky during a rainstorm are fish and frogs. Jellyfish once fell from the sky in England.

In 1783, a volcanic eruption in Iceland temporarily blocked out the sun over Europe.

Antarctica is the only continent where pumpkins cannot grow.

Antarctica has only
one ATM.

Very tall buildings naturally
lean toward the sun.

Plants that are not watered will cry for help; a thirsty plant will make a high-pitched sound that is too high for humans to hear.

There are more stars than all the grains of sand on Earth.

It takes twelve people twenty hours to make one Oscar statuette.

Toto the dog was paid $125 per week while filming *The Wizard of Oz*.

Professional ballerinas use about twelve pairs of toe shoes per week.

Pinocchio was made of pine.

In the oldest known version of the Cinderella fairy tale, her slippers were made of gold, not glass.

A woman once received a box in the mail with a human brain in it.

Reading about yawning makes most people yawn.

Human thighbones are stronger than concrete.

The four most dangerous steps in a staircase are the two steps at the top and the two at the bottom.

Baboons cannot throw overhand.

Chickens lay more eggs
when pop music is played.

The world's biggest dog weighed 282 pounds.

Chocolate was once believed to cure stomachaches.

The Incas used to wash their children's hair with urine as a remedy for head lice.

Birds can't sweat.

More toilets flush during halftime of the Super Bowl than at any other time of the year.

Termites are the largest producers of farts.

The largest snowflakes that
ever fell on Earth were
fifteen inches in diameter.

A thirteen-year-old boy
once found a tooth growing
out of his left foot.

ABOUT THE AUTHOR

Noel Botham is chairman and founding member of the Useless Information Society. He and the rest of his team lurk mostly around London. He is the author of *The Book of Useless Information, The Ultimate Book of Useless Information, The Best Book of Useless Information Ever, The World's Greatest Book of Useless Information,* and *The Amazing Book of Useless Information.*

ABOUT THE ILLUSTRATOR

Travis Nichols is a writer, illustrator, Texan, and cartoonist living in New York. He is the author and illustrator of *The Monster Doodle Book, Matthew Meets the Man,* and other books for kids and post-kids. He enjoys meteorites and eating watermelon over the sink. He can be found online at www.ilikeapplejuice.com.